D1712927

COUNTRY PROFILES

BELGIUM

BY CHRIS BOWMAN

BELLWETHER MEDIA • MINNEAPOLIS, MN

Blastoff! Discovery launches
a new mission: reading to learn.
Filled with facts and features, each
book offers you an exciting new
world to explore!

This edition first published in 2020 by Bellwether Media, Inc.

No part of this publication may be reproduced in whole or in part
without written permission of the publisher.
For information regarding permission, write to Bellwether Media, Inc.,
Attention: Permissions Department,
6012 Blue Circle Drive, Minnetonka, MN 55343.

Library of Congress Cataloging-in-Publication Data

Names: Bowman, Chris, 1990- author.
Title: Belgium / by Chris Bowman.
Description: Minneapolis, MN : Bellwether Media, Inc., 2020. |
    Series: Blastoff! discovery : country profiles | Includes bibliographical
    references and index. | Audience: Ages 7-13 | Audience:
    Grades 4-6 | Summary: ""Engaging images accompany
    information about Belgium. The combination of high-interest subject
    matter and narrative text is intended for students in grades 3
    through 8" – Provided by publisher.
Identifiers: LCCN 2019034856 (print) | LCCN 2019034857 (ebook)
    | ISBN 9781644871652 (library binding) |
    ISBN9781618918413 (ebook)
Subjects: LCSH: Belgium–Juvenile literature.
Classification: LCC DH418 .B68 2020 (print) | LCC DH418 (ebook)
    | DDC 949.3–dc23
LC record available at https://lccn.loc.gov/2019034856
LC ebook record available at https://lccn.loc.gov/2019034857

Editor: Rebecca Sabelko   Designer: Brittany McIntosh

Printed in the United States of America, North Mankato, MN.

TABLE OF CONTENTS

BELFRY
BRUGES

A family steps off the train in the charming city of Bruges. They head to the Lake of Love to relax after their long journey. Next, the family admires the **medieval** buildings as they wander the city's cobblestone streets. Soon they reach the **Quay** of the Rosary. They stop to snap a photo of this famous view of the city.

STEPPING UP
There are 366 steps to the top of Bruges's Belfry.

OTHER TOP SITES

ATOMIUM

GRAND-PLACE OF BRUSSELS

GRAVENSTEEN CASTLE

HOGE KEMPEN NATIONAL PARK

The family continues to Burg Square where they admire many grand buildings. Then they head to the Market Square. It is home to busy cafes and the towering Belfry. In this historic city, the family feels like they are in a fairy tale!

LOCATION

North

W E

S

NORTH
SEA

Belgium is a small country in northwestern Europe. This wide country covers 11,787 square miles (30,528 square kilometers). Brussels is the capital city. It is also the capital city of the European Union. It lies near the middle of the country.

Despite its small size, Belgium shares borders with four countries. The Netherlands borders Belgium to the north. Germany and Luxembourg are its neighbors to the east. Belgium shares a long border with France along the south and west. The cold waters of the North Sea wash along Belgium's northwestern shores.

THE
NETHERLANDS

ANTWERP

GHENT

GERMANY

BELGIUM

BRUSSELS

LIÈGE

CHARLEROI

LUXEMBOURG

FRANCE

LANDSCAPE AND CLIMATE

Much of Belgium's land is flat and low-lying. A series of **canals** and walls helps protect the land from flooding near the coast. Belgium's central location provides most of the land with a **temperate** climate. Rain and fog are common.

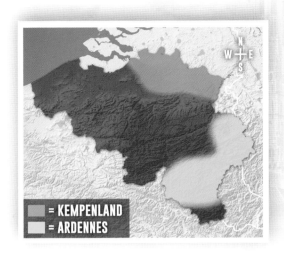

= KEMPENLAND
= ARDENNES

KEMPENLAND

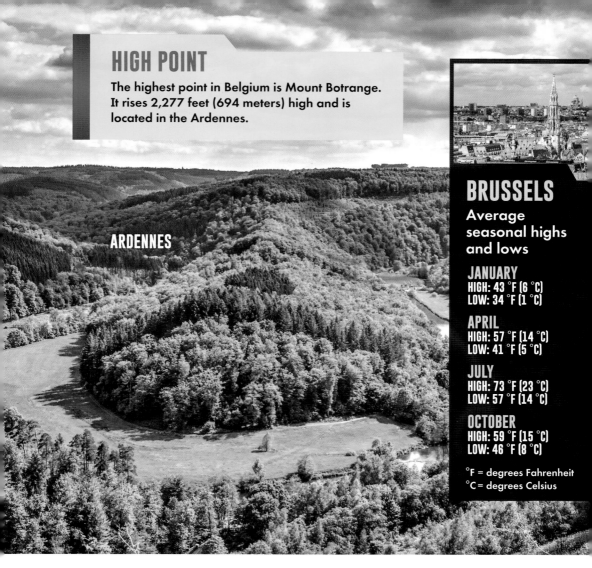

HIGH POINT

The highest point in Belgium is Mount Botrange. It rises 2,277 feet (694 meters) high and is located in the Ardennes.

ARDENNES

BRUSSELS

Average seasonal highs and lows

JANUARY
HIGH: 43 °F (6 °C)
LOW: 34 °F (1 °C)

APRIL
HIGH: 57 °F (14 °C)
LOW: 41 °F (5 °C)

JULY
HIGH: 73 °F (23 °C)
LOW: 57 °F (14 °C)

OCTOBER
HIGH: 59 °F (15 °C)
LOW: 46 °F (8 °C)

°F = degrees Fahrenheit
°C = degrees Celsius

The Kempenland region is located in the northeast. It has many mines and some pine forests. Central **plateaus** cover the middle of Belgium. This region is home to the country's biggest cities. The land becomes hilly in the southeast Ardennes region. This area has a **continental** climate and includes the majority of Belgium's forests.

9

Belgium was once covered by thick forests. However, much of this land has been cleared for cities and farmland. Because of this, Belgium has relatively few wild animals. Most of Belgium's animals live in the Ardennes.

The country has many wild boars. They roam the forests in search of food. Lynx and wildcats are growing in numbers. Wolves are also returning to Belgium. Deer call the country's forests and fields home. In the lowlands, birds such as sandpipers, snipes, and Eurasian woodcocks are common.

GRAY WOLF

WILDCAT

SNIPE

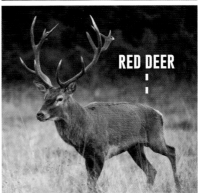

RED DEER

SANDPIPER

WILD BOAR AND PIGLETS

WILD BOAR

Life Span: 10 years
Red List Status: least concern

wild boar range =

LEAST CONCERN	NEAR THREATENED	VULNERABLE	ENDANGERED	CRITICALLY ENDANGERED	EXTINCT IN THE WILD	EXTINCT

THIRD TONGUE

A small number of Belgians primarily speak German. These people generally live in eastern Belgium, near the German border.

Most Belgians live in cities in the northern parts of the country. The majority of people in Belgium are of Belgian **descent**. However, some people have moved from other countries and still identify with other **ethnic** groups. Many **migrants** travel to Belgium seeking safety and better living conditions.

Belgium is often split into two main **cultural** regions. Northern Belgium is called Flanders. The Flemish people speak Dutch. Belgians from the south, or Wallonia, generally speak French. People from the area around Brussels speak both languages. Many people in both regions are Roman Catholic, the country's most popular religion.

FAMOUS FACE

Name: **Eden Hazard**
Birthday: **January 7, 1991**
Hometown: **La Louvière, Belgium**
Famous for: **A star winger and midfielder for Real Madrid who also led the Belgium men's national team to a third-place finish in the 2018 FIFA World Cup**

SPEAK DUTCH

ENGLISH	DUTCH	HOW TO SAY IT
hello	hallo	HAH-low
goodbye	tot ziens	toht zeens
please	alstublieft	ahls-tew-BLEEFT
thank you	dank u	DAHNK ew
yes	ja	YAA
no	nee	NAY

BRUSSELS

Belgians commonly live in single-family homes. But people live in apartment buildings as well. The Belgian government offers programs to help low-income families find affordable places to live.

BRUGES

14

BY ANY OTHER NAME

Bruxelles Nord
Brussel Noord →

Many cities in Belgium have different names in French and Dutch. Road signs are usually written in the main language of the region. But signs in Brussels often have directions in both languages.

GHENT

There are many ways to travel around Belgium. Trains regularly run between Belgian cities. They also connect the country to other places around Europe. Many Belgians also own cars, and highways are another fast way to get around. For shorter trips around the city, bicycles are common.

THE FUNNIES

Comic strips are an important part of Belgium's culture. The country is home to many famous comic strip characters, such as Tintin and the Smurfs.

Most Belgians find it important to be on time. Belgians often prefer to meet up with friends or family in public places. Cities usually have many parks and public squares. Cafes and restaurants often have outdoor seating available.

On a daily basis, Belgians wear clothing similar to other western European countries. But people often wear **traditional** clothing for weddings and special celebrations. Men often wear smocks and berets. Women wear huntress dresses.

Belgian children often begin preschool when they are about 3 years old. Students move on to six years of primary school at the age of 6. Most students then continue on to six years of secondary school. Belgians often continue their education at one of the country's colleges or universities.

About four out of five Belgians have **service jobs**. These often include working in health care, **tourism**, or the government. Workers commonly **manufacture** steel products, chemical products, and foods. Belgium also has a small number of farmers who raise livestock.

BARISTA

OIL FACTORY WORKER

SOCCER

Soccer is the most popular sport in Belgium. Many of the country's biggest cities have their own professional teams. Belgians also follow the national teams closely. Cycling is another favorite sport. Many people take part in local cycling clubs. Belgium also hosts a number of big races throughout the spring and summer.

CYCLING

Belgians typically like to spend time outside during vacation. Families visit beaches in the northwest. Activities such as swimming and canoeing are popular. Hiking trails in the southern forests also draw many visitors.

HIKING

KRACHTBAL

Krachtbal, which means powerball, is a game played between two teams of four players. It is usually played on a large field.

What You Need:
- a large ball
- a playing field

Instructions:

1. Mark the goal lines, free throw lines, and center line with cones or other objects.

2. Players throw the ball with both hands over their heads. A "neck throw" is when the player faces forward to throw the ball. A "back throw" is when the player faces backwards to throw the ball.

3. Points are scored when the ball lands on the ground of the other team's goal. "Neck throws" score one point, and "back throws" score two points.

4. The team with the ball gets three throws to move it up the field. They first throw from the team's free throw line. The next two throws come from where the ball lands on the last throw. If the other team catches the ball, it is their turn to throw. Passes can only be made backwards.

5. The game is played in two 25-minute periods. The team with the most points at the end wins!

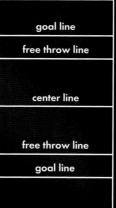

| goal line |
| free throw line |
| center line |
| free throw line |
| goal line |

FRY FANS

Many people think fries were invented in Belgium instead of France. They were likely first made in southern Belgium, where French is mainly spoken.

Belgium is famous for a handful of different foods. *Moules frites*, or mussels with french fries, is a popular meal. French fries served in paper cones are also a favorite street food. Mayonnaise is poured on top of the fries, and a small fork is used to eat them.

Waffles are another favorite snack in Belgium. They are usually eaten plain or with powdered sugar. However, shops usually have fruits, chocolate, whipped cream, and other treats to top them off. Belgium is also known for its chocolates. Many cities have several chocolate shops that offer a variety of treats.

WAFFLES

CHOCOLATES

FRENCH FRIES

Belgians are famous for frying their fries twice for the right flavor and texture. Have an adult help you make these easy oven fries.

Ingredients:
2 pounds of Russet or
    Yukon Gold potatoes
3 tablespoons olive oil
salt, to taste
mayonnaise

Steps:
1. Wash, peel, and cut the potatoes into small slices.
2. In a large bowl, cover the potato slices with hot tap water. Let sit for 10 minutes.
3. Preheat the oven to 450 degrees Fahrenheit (232 degrees Celsius).
4. Coat a large baking pan with 1 1/2 tablespoons of olive oil.
5. Drain the water from the bowl. Use a clean towel to dry the potato slices.
6. Drizzle the remaining oil over the potato slices.
7. Spread the potato slices out on the baking pan, then sprinkle with salt. Bake for about 20 minutes.

Christianity plays a central role in many of Belgium's holidays. In the days leading up to Lent, the Carnival of Binche features a parade of people dressed in masks and bright outfits to ward off evil. During Lent, the Laetare festival of Stavelot includes a parade with costumes, fireworks, and music.

CARNIVAL OF BINCHE

STOP AND SMELL THE CARPET

Every two years, Brussels decorates its Grand-Place with a large "carpet" of flowers in mid-August. The designs usually have a theme and are put together by around 100 people in less than eight hours. In 2018, the theme was Mexico!

FLOWER CARPET 2018

Every three years, the city of Ypres hosts the Festival of Cats. On "Cats Wednesday," the city's bell rings, and a parade leads to the bell tower. Plush cats are thrown from the tower onto the crowd below. Those lucky enough to catch one make a wish. Belgians love their unique celebrations!

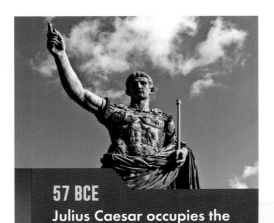

1914
Germany invades Belgium in World War I

1922
Belgium takes over Germany's colonies in Rwanda and Burundi following World War I

57 BCE
Julius Caesar occupies the area that is now Belgium, placing it under Roman rule

1830 CE
Belgium declares independence from the Netherlands

1940
Belgium is invaded by Germany in World War II

1908
Belgium establishes the Belgian Congo colony in Africa

2016

Terrorist attacks in Brussels take the lives of dozens of people and leave hundreds injured

1962

Rwanda and Burundi receive independence from Belgium

1958

The Netherlands, Luxembourg, and Belgium form an economic union that allows for goods and services to move between the countries for free

2002

Belgium switches its currency from the Belgian franc to the Euro

BELGIUM FACTS

Official Name: Kingdom of Belgium

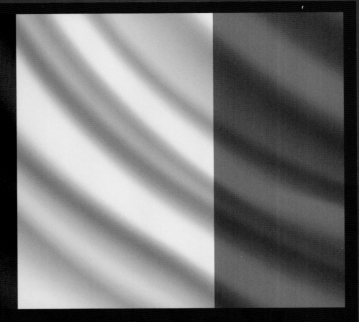

Flag of Belgium: The Belgian flag has three vertical stripes of equal width. Black is on the left, yellow is in the middle, and red is on the right. The flag's design was inspired by the French flag's vertical stripes.

Area: 11,787 square miles
(30,528 square kilometers)

Capital City: Brussels

Important Cities: Antwerp, Ghent, Charleroi, Liège

Population:
11,570,762 (July 2018)

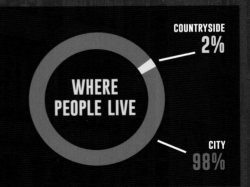

WHERE PEOPLE LIVE

COUNTRYSIDE
2%

CITY
98%

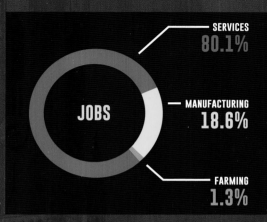

SERVICES
80.1%

JOBS

MANUFACTURING
18.6%

FARMING
1.3%

Main Exports:

chemicals

machinery

metals

foods

diamonds

National Holiday:
Belgian National Day (July 21)

Main Languages:
Dutch, French, and German

Form of Government:
federal parliamentary democracy
under a constitutional monarchy

Title for Country Leaders:
prime minister (head of government),
king (head of state)

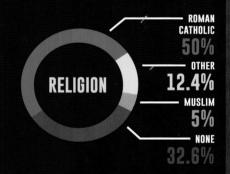

RELIGION

ROMAN CATHOLIC
50%

OTHER
12.4%

MUSLIM
5%

NONE
32.6%

Unit of Money:
Euro

GLOSSARY

canals—waterways for boats

continental—relating to a relatively dry climate with very cold winters and very hot summers

cultural—relating to the beliefs, arts, and ways of life in a place or society

descent—related to a person or group of people who lived at an earlier time

ethnic—related to a group of people who share customs and an identity

manufacture—to make products, often with machines

medieval—relating to the Middle Ages; the Middle Ages were a period of European history from about 500 CE to 1500 CE.

migrants—people who have moved to a new place for work or who have been forced to leave their home

plateaus—areas of flat, raised land

quay—a platform next to water used for loading and unloading ships

service jobs—jobs that perform tasks for people or businesses

temperate—associated with a mild climate that does not have extreme heat or cold

tourism—the business of people traveling to visit other places

traditional—related to customs, ideas, or beliefs handed down from one generation to the next

TO LEARN MORE

AT THE LIBRARY

Ainsley, Dominic J. *Belgium*. Broomall, Pa.: Mason Crest, 2019.

Klepeis, Alicia Z. *The Netherlands*. Minneapolis, Minn.: Bellwether Media, 2020.

Rechner, Amy. *France*. Minneapolis, Minn.: Bellwether Media, 2018.

ON THE WEB

FACTSURFER

Factsurfer.com gives you a safe, fun way to find more information.

1. Go to www.factsurfer.com.

2. Enter "Belgium" into the search box and click 🔍.

3. Select your book cover to see a list of related web sites.

INDEX